Images of
Carlisle

The Cumberland News

Images of Carlisle

The Breedon Books
Publishing Company
Derby

First published in Great Britain by
The Breedon Books Publishing Company Limited
Breedon House, 44 Friar Gate, Derby, DE1 1DA.
1999

ISBN 1 85983 154 0

Printed and bound by Butler & Tanner Ltd., Selwood
Printing Works, Caxton Road, Frome, Somerset.

Colour separations and jacket printing by Green Shires
Group Ltd, Leicester.

Contents

Acknowledgments

The Cumberland News would like to thank the following who have contributed photographs: Mr and Mrs A. Morland; Mrs G. Oscroft; Mr Edwin Mason; Mr A. Lewthwaite; Mrs Annie Bell; Mr W. Stoddart; Mr D. B. Jessiman; Mr C. Mackenzie; Mrs J. L. Jolly; Mrs A. Pagin; Miss Anna Hope; Mrs Audrey Bell; Mr R. A. Styth; Mrs E. Latimer; Mr E. S. Graham; Mrs Carol Burgess; Mr A. Donoghue; Mr G. W. Robinson; Mrs Norma Brock; Mr Edward Lightfoot; Mr J. Graham; Mr and Mrs D. Whitfield; Mrs E. McKie; Mrs D. Smithson; Mrs M. Crawford; Mrs S. Wheatley; Mrs K. Duffy; Mr Peter Leslie; Mr R. M. Upton; Mr Ray Saunders; Mrs C. Ramsay; Mr Peter Brock; Mr John Zeller; Mrs M. B. McKay; Mrs Patricia Kelton; Mr J. D. H. Chapman; Mrs Eileen Slack; Mrs Jennifer Sherdley; Mrs Eileen Robson; Calum Scott-Buccleugh; Mrs Mary Jackson.

Most of the photographs in this book have been taken by *Cumberland News* staff photographers since 1952:
Bill Walker; Maureen Cowie (née Main); Jim Turner; Peter Dunn; Laurie Kemp; Mike Scott; John Watson; Loftus Brown; Phil Rigby; Eleanor Mason; Stewart Blair; Ian Cooper.

Foreword

CARLISLE has always been an important place for people to live, built on high ground, almost surrounded by rivers. This natural defensive site, overlooking crossing points on the rivers, has been settled from an early period.

Excavations in Botchergate in 1999 have shown that the Roman town of Luguvalium was much larger than originally thought. Further archaeological work beside Carlisle Castle has given new evidence for the layout of the Roman fort, first constructed in 71AD. All this established Carlisle's position as the administrative centre for the Roman Wall.

As a fortification on the border with Scotland, Carlisle was an important medieval walled city, the only one in Cumbria. When this role ceased in 1603, with the union of the Crowns, it was suggested that Carlisle could become a textile city: this it did, but not until the 18th century. With three rivers flowing through the suburbs of the city, power could be provided for the machinery necessary in textile manufacture and water for the various finishing processes. One textile firm in Carlisle employed 8,000 hand-loom weavers at the height of production, at the beginning of the 19th century.

To help with the expansion of Carlisle, the city walls were partly demolished in 1811 and a canal linked the city with the sea in 1823. This waterway brought many of the raw materials for manufacturers and provided a vital route for exports. Materials imported, such as Welsh slate and Baltic timber, helped in the rapid development of the city in the 1840s and 1850s, the population doubling in that period.

The coming of railways to Carlisle in 1836 helped to shape the city. As a railway centre, Carlisle station is where Scotland met England, accommodating seven different companies. Each company had its own engine shed and goods facilities, occupying vast areas. At one period, almost a third of the working population in the city was employed by the railways. It was railways that brought other industries to Carlisle.

All the working population had to be housed and new estates in the late 19th century expanded the city into Currock, Denton Holme, Newtown, Wigton Road, London Road and Warwick Road. Stanwix, Upperby, Botcherby and Harraby all became part of an ever-growing city in 1912.

Much of the older slum property was replaced by council housing in large estates, surrounding the older core, before and after the war. This happened to such an extent that the city's boundary was again enlarged in 1951. Post-war legislation has seen the establishment of industrial estates which separate where people live from where they work.

With the area considered 'safe' from enemy bombing in the war, Carlisle became the centre for military training and maintenance, for the RAF and Army. Numerous aerodromes surrounded Carlisle, with a munitions depot on the outskirts; three army camps were also constructed. Prisoner of war camps were not far away.

Although Carlisle was not bombed, many of the older buildings in the city centre have gone to be replaced by shopping developments such as the award-winning Lanes and new roads. Enough of the old city survives to make this a tourist destination.

In 1950, who would have thought that there would come a time when you could not buy a Buck's shirt or a pint of State beer; that there would be no dividend stamps, or even a Co-op in Botchergate and that you could not travel to Silloth for a holiday by railway.

It is the second half of the 20th century which has seen the most rapid change. Fortunately, more photographs were taken at this time than in any previous period, not just newspaper photographs, but those taken by ordinary people. The diversity of images showing these changes can be seen in this book.

My thanks are due to all those who have made this book possible, from readers to photographers and printers, and none more so than Jim Turner, *The Cumberland News*'s own chief photographer for 11 years and a photographer with the paper for 48 years. Thanks to Jim's 'retirement' in 1999, he has been able to work non-stop on this valuable and beautifully produced book.

Keith Sutton
Editor
The Cumberland News

CHAPTER ONE
Our Changing City

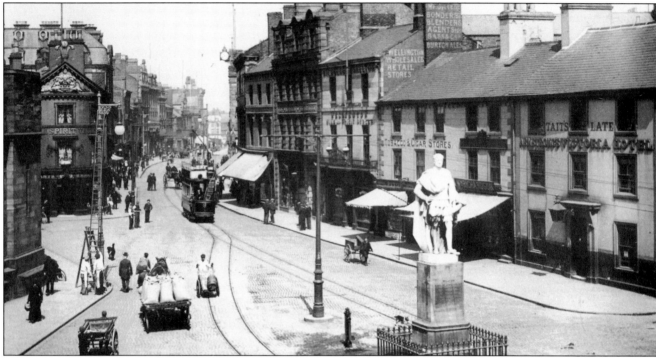

A statue of William, Earl of Lonsdale and Lord Lieutenant of Cumberland and Westmorland stands guard to English Street in this view from the Courts.

An early picture of Carlisle looking down Botchergate as a tram approaches the city centre, travelling between the old Red Lion Hotel on the left and the former Midland Bank on the right.

Seen from Scotch Street, this picture from 1960 shows the site to be used for the new Civic Centre.

In 1961 the last wall was demolished to clear the way for construction of the Civic Centre.

Looking from Rickergate, the new Civic Centre starts to rise in 1961.

The completed Civic Centre seen in 1968 from the northern entrance to the city across Eden Bridges. Hardwicke Circus roundabout has still not been built as traffic merges between Lowther Street (left) and Scotch Street.

Shops along Lowther Street, before demolition for The Lanes development.

Looking along Globe Lane towards Lowther Street at the start of demolition of the site for The Lanes development.

Houses between Lowther Street and Scotch Street that had not been lived in for some time are demolished for the start of The Lanes development.

A quiet day shows off The Lanes shopping centre and market cross looking towards Scotch Street.

From the crane that moved materials for the construction of The Lanes shopping complex this view in 1983 shows the layout of the foundations looking towards the Civic Centre and Stanwix.

The Duke of Gloucester unveils a plaque on the ground at the official opening of The Lanes shopping complex.

Although close to the centre of the city, this early photograph of the walk along the River Eden in Bitts Park looks very rural.

The lrishgate Tavern in 1963, later demolished to make way for the inner ring road to the west of the city centre.

Looking west along Annetwell Street at the junction with Castle Street, the former Salvation Army Citadel stands on the right at the entrance to the castle.

Demolition of houses in Barwise Nook, Willow Holme, during 1966 as workmen remove tiles from the roofs. In the background is the Power Station.

Cecil Street Methodist Church, built 1852, had its last service in 1966 when it was demolished to make way for an extension to the new telephone exchange.

The last service in Cecil Street Methodist Church, 1966.

Blackfriars Street runs behind English Street and is now a busy entrance for Tesco's car park. Towards the far end is the rear of Marks and Spencer and the food hall.

A thriving Scotch Street in 1966 showing on the left Potter's the tobacconists with City Hairdressers above.

The new automatic telephone exchange which opened in Cecil Street in 1957.

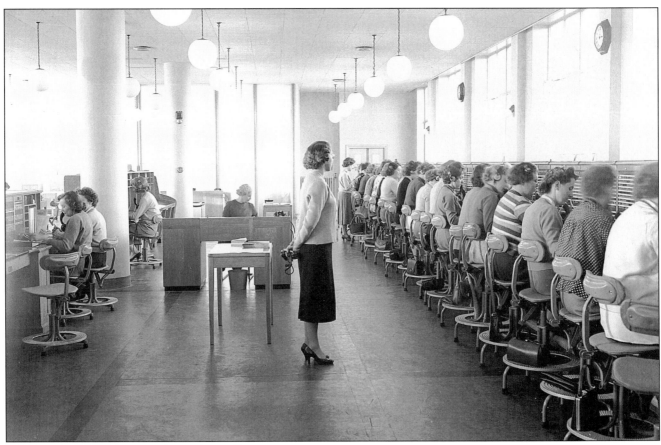

Inside the new telephone exchange in Cecil Street.

Opposite the automatic telephone exchange the site is cleared for a new building to house new equipment.

A city centre view in 1958 when traffic and pedestrians still used the area together. On the left is the market cross, the Town Hall is on the right and in the background Carlisle Cathedral.

Looking towards the city centre, this photograph shows the Viaduct car park under construction in 1957.

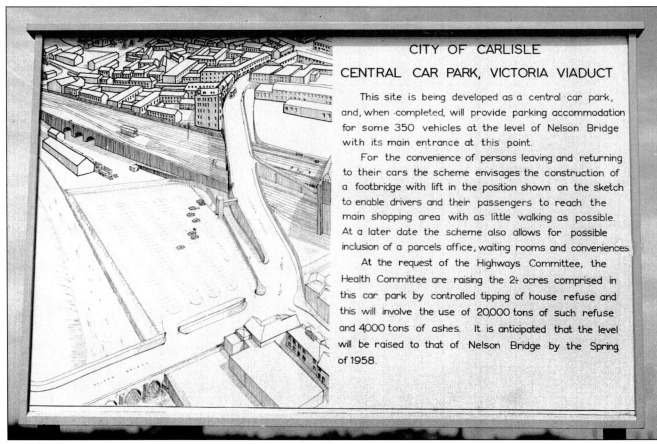

An explanation notice at the site of the Viaduct car park in 1957.

Her Majesty's Theatre in Lowther Street just before demolition in 1980.

Inside Her Majesty's Theatre after the demolition had started with the stage just visible on the right and the circle still intact above.

Looking along Spencer Street towards Hardwicke Circus in 1970 as houses in Victoria Place are demolished to make way for the inner ring road.

The YMCA in Fisher Street, Carlisle, in 1952 before changes were made to the front.

This 1958 photograph of the Viaduct shows the former Viaduct Hotel and Queens Hall which were demolished to make way for a Tesco store.

The Palace cinema, Botchergate, in 1958.

Staff at the closure of the Palace cinema.

The Botchergate cinema, re-named the Gaumont and then the Odeon, pictured in 1968.

The foyer of the Odeon cinema.

A queue of local youngsters at the opening of the Argyle cinema at Harraby in 1956. It later became the Cosmo ballroom.

Viewed in 1972 from the crane high above the construction, the early building of the extension to the Cumberland Infirmary can be seen below.

Looking towards the curtained screen in the Argyle cinema which was opened at Harraby in 1956.

The completed extension to the Cumberland Infirmary.

A busy work site at the Sands in 1983 during construction of the Sport and Leisure Centre.

The Sands Leisure Centre today used extensively for sports, concerts, as a fitness centre and a venue for private functions.

Labour leader Neil Kinnock (right) opened the new £4.5 million Sands Leisure Centre in 1985. He is accompanied by the Mayor and Mayoress of Carlisle, Ian and Pat Stockdale, and the Town Clerk, Ron Wilson, as he looks around the foyer.

CHAPTER TWO

Around and About

An early photograph on Stanwix Bank, showing thatched cottages on the junction between Scotland Road on the left and Brampton Road. A sign on the end of one of the cottages gives the distances to eight towns on the two routes.

An early photograph for the family album from around 1911 of children in East Norfolk Street, Denton Holme.

A crowd gathers in 1945 to watch the demolition of an air-raid shelter which was built for protection during World War Two at the junction of Lund Crescent and Lediard Avenue opposite Currock House.

Now a small car park just off Caldewgate, Paddy's Market is pictured in 1954 as traders set out their wares. In the foreground a carousel is set up for the amusement of children. The main road is still cobbled and the far end of the view looks more open now since the demolition of some of the buildings.

Looking along the mill stream that runs through Shaddongate, Brewery Row which is pictured in 1959 stands on the site of what is now a small trading estate.

This was Shaddongate in 1966 looking towards Dixon's Chimney, very much a residential area until major demolition two years later.

Back yard party time in 1957 for Kenneth Armstrong who was celebrating his birthday.

Looking along Shaddongate towards Dalston Road, demolition made room for a wider road and new commercial buildings in 1968.

With the surrounding area still unfinished, these shops at Central Avenue had just been completed in 1956 to serve the new housing area at Harraby. When they were built they looked out on to the new Argyle Cinema.

Morton Manor, home of Sir Robert Chance and family, as it was in 1961, seven years before it was turned into Morton Community Centre after being handed over to the city council.

The audience at the opening of Morton Community Centre in 1967.

Anyone for boxing, snooker or table tennis? Arriving at Currock House Community Centre in the 1960s to spend an evening of activites with friends at the youth club.

Children at play chase a ball down Princess Street at St Nicholas before demolition of the houses and subsequent development of a business site.

The northern outskirts of the city at Kingstown photographed in 1961 shows the A7 to Longtown on the right and the A74 to Glasgow forking off to the left. The cottage on the left has now been converted into a branch of the Midland Bank following road changes and the building of the M6 motorway junction.

Looking along Wigton Road towards Carlisle in 1969, the footbridge outside Morton School is being erected across the busy road leading into the city from the west. This provided safe access to the school for pupils living on the other side of the main road.

Canon Patrick Begley, who died in 1987, is pictured on top of the new St Margaret Mary's Church, Upperby, in 1962 as he looks over his parish. He devoted 40 years of his life to the church and was a well-known figure in the city. In 1968 he became the first Roman Catholic priest to preach in Carlisle Cathedral since the Reformation.

The Revd Lowther, the first vicar at St Elisabeth's new church in Harraby, joins workmen at the topping off ceremony in 1967 as the exterior building work comes to an end prior to the consecration later that year.

A prominent landmark in Caldewgate, Holy Trinity Church on the junction of Church Street and Port Road is pictured here in 1969 when it was still a thriving church.

Looking back towards the city, the demolition work started on Holy Trinity Church in 1981. George Earl (left) and a colleague are seen on the tower which was the highest part of the building. Demolition of the whole church was necessary because of the poor state of repair.

Standing on the skyline near Harraby, the Hilltop Motor Hotel is almost ready for opening in 1970. The original building was owned by the railway companies and provided stop-over dormitory accommodation for locomotive staff in times when it took too long to work back to their home base in one shift.

Morton West on the right of Wigton Road is still a farm and fields, in this aerial photograph taken in 1968. Looking away from the city, Orton Road cuts across the bottom with Inglewood Crescent in the lower centre. The area is now fully developed with housing, a garage and Morton School.

A misty morning in Charlotte Street 1973, looking towards Dixon's chimney. The terraces of houses were demolished two years later and replaced with flats for the elderly and garden areas.

Party time with a cake too, but not really a celebration. This group had a final get-together in 1975 before they had to leave their houses in Charlotte Street which were scheduled for demolition.

CHAPTER THREE
Carlisle at Work

An early photograph in Castle Street, Carlisle, near to Bullough's with a lane leading to Carlyle Court. The shop on the left is a painter and decorators, next, a leather cutting warehouse and the large shop, in the centre, is for the sale of glass, china and fancy goods.

Thomas Wilkinson outside his family butcher's shop at 74 London Road in the early 1920s. Notice the pigs' heads and the sheep still with their fleeces on.

A newsagent and tobacconist's shop in Blackwell Road, owned by J. Morland.

Mabel Mackenzie outside her corner shop in Shaddongate, 1959.

Until the late 1950s, the Hirings took place around Carlisle Cross each year when employers and those looking for work would gather to hopefully strike up a deal. These farm workers reminisce as they wait for an approach.

Marks and Spencer assistants who took part in a mannequin parade in 1954 to show off the goods available in the store.

An early horse-drawn road sweeper is seen about to leave Carlisle Corporation yard in the 1930s.

A prizewinning horse-drawn float leaves Ferguson's factory at Holme Head for a May Day procession in the 1930s.

Seen in 1954, these railway horses were used to deliver goods around the city from their base in Crown Street. In the background can be seen the Coulthards building now occupied by Carlisle Glass.

The 14 MU radio workshops at number 3 site, photographed in 1960, were part of the large RAF operation to the north of the city which had supplied spares for the service since World War Two. The whole site was closed in September 1996 with the work transferred to other parts of the country.

An original letter head of Cavaghan Collin and Gray from 1913.

Cavaghan and Gray, the meat processing company in London Road, seen in the 1960s. They have now developed into one of the largest and most sophisticated fresh food producers in the country serving such stores as Marks and Spencer with recipe dish meals.

Ladies work on their machines in the main shirt assembly section at the Atlas Works of Robert R. Buck and Sons Ltd, Nelson Street.

Screen printing at Stead McAlpin and Sons Ltd, in the 1960s, producing high-class furnishings at their Cummersdale works.

Todd's Mill in Junction Street looks almost the same as it does today in this 1967 photograph. Dixon's Chimney is one of Carlisle's best-known landmarks, built in 13 months by local builder Richard Wright in 1836 working from the inside. It was originally 305 feet high, and said at the time to be the highest in the world. Since then it has been reduced in height twice and has recently been strengthened by the fitting of steel bands. The mill itself closed in the mid 1970s and now houses individual small business units.

Clearance in 1967 for a new Courtaulds factory to be built on a large site on the corner of Blencowe Street and Nelson Street in Denton Holme.

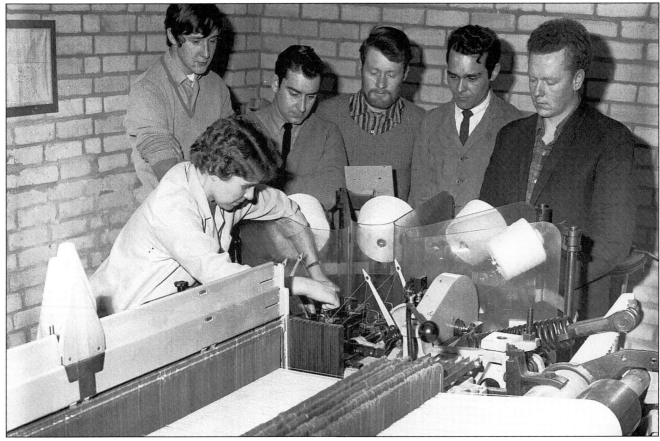

Weavers for the new Courtaulds factory are trained in 1968 ready for the opening of the factory. The factory closed down at the end of the 1980s.

The construction of the Pirelli factory in the outskirts of the city on Dalston Road is well under way in 1968. The long shed on the left is part of the tyre building plant. When production started, there was also a small department making slippers.

One of the stations in the tyre production assembly at Pirelli which opened in 1969.

Workers in the slipper department at the new Pirelli factory show off the finished goods during the early days of production.

The entrance to Cowans Sheldon, the crane makers known worldwide, who had their works in London Road. The site was demolished in 1989 and developed as the St Nicholas Gate shopping area with its own car parking.

In 1960, Cowans Sheldon and Co, of St Nicholas, were constructing this 4-ton electric travelling grabbing crane among other projects in the huge workshop.

A 1960s industrial scene looking from Caldewgate towards the gas works. The signal box and semaphore signals show the city's railway heritage.

In 1966 Rickerby's showroom and workshops moved to new building land on Currock Road from their previous site in town at Mary Street. The land has since been further developed for businesses and a motor service station.

Part of the showroom of agricultural suppliers Rickerby's after they moved to their new premises on Currock Road in 1966.

Earl Street Mart, off Warwick Road in 1969, one of two city cattle marts owned by Harrison and Hetherington. The new Crown Court building is now situated on this site, both Earl Street and Botchergate marts having moved to Rosehill.

This aerial view of Rosehill industrial estate shows the Harrison and Hetherington mart just before the official opening in 1974. The road in the foreground is the extension of Warwick Road to the motorway and the building between it and the mart was the County Motors garage now owned by Lloyd Rover. The rest of the estate seen on the right is now developed, with much of the area taken by motor dealerships.

Willie Whitelaw, MP for Penrith and the Border, opens the new Harrison and Hetherington mart at Rosehill in 1974. The mart replaced those at Botchergate and Earl Street, both in the city centre. The area in Botchergate was purchased by the city council to build an inner ring road that never materialised further than Spencer Street.

Bob Jenkins, back right, supervising a delivery of lamb to the Pioneer Meat Store in Fisher Street. Note the layout of the narrow road to give a smoother ride for horse-drawn vehicles from earlier times. It was in 1974 that Pioneer Foods, like Harrison and Hetherington, moved their business to Rosehill to include the Shepherd's Inn banqueting hall.

Pictured from the air in 1998, this is the Kingstown Industrial Estate to the north of the city, seen from above the Posthouse Forte Hotel.

One of the large businesses operating from Kingstown Industrial Estate is Eddie Stobart Ltd. Seen here with one of his 800 vehicles is chairman Edward Stobart, whose company has its own fan club and a shop in the city selling souvenirs.

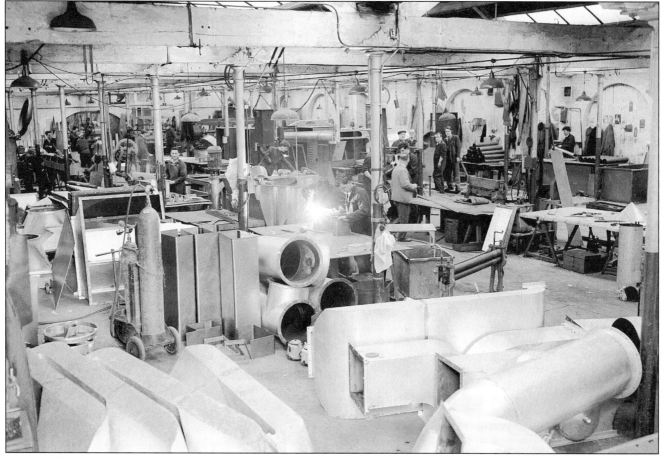

A view of the general sheet metal and plate works in 1960 of James Bendall and Sons Ltd, Albion Works, in London Road.

Seen here in 1969 in their shop premises at the corner of Lowther Street and East Tower Street, Thomas Graham were suppliers of tools and building trades material, and are now iron and steel suppliers based in Shaddongate.

E. T. Roberts on the corner of The Crescent and Warwick Road were one of the largest city music shops in the 1960s. Apart from records, they have here on display in 1969 radiograms and television sets.

The Silver Grill in English Street (now Boots) was a busy bakery and coffee shop during the day and in the evenings a popular venue for dinner dances. Held throughout the winter months by local companies and various organisations, they often seated 300 people. Part of the original Boots shop can be seen on the right.

In 1966 when Carlisle had a traditional covered market, small stallholders from the country would join the regular traders on a Saturday to sell their produce.

Fruit and vegetables displayed on one of the regular stalls in the covered market in 1968.

The covered market was re-designed for 1990, and is currently under yet another rebuilding project which has involved splitting it into two floors.

Asda was the first out of town supermarket, opening at Parkhouse in 1987 after an earlier public inquiry following fears by local traders.

Farming came to the centre of Carlisle early in 1998 to highlight the farming crisis prior to the national Countryside Rally held in London a few days later. This was preceded by thousands of beacons being lit across the country as farmers who were worried about their future and the rural economy united to show their plight to the government, demonstrating about the low prices for beef, sheep and milk.

CHAPTER FOUR
Railway City

Pictured in 1954 from the footbridge at Upperby rail sheds in Carlisle, Diesels 10,000 and 10,001 are pictured on the main line south as they stop for a driver changeover. They ran together and were the first non-steam locomotives on the main line in this country.

Steam and Diesel together at Kingmoor in 1956 before the demise of steam as a main locomotive. The new Deltic diesel arrived in August for passenger and goods trials between Carlisle and Skipton, its first Carlisle driver William Kelly from Denton Holme.

The Caledonian, a high-speed train that ran one return journey each day between London and Glasgow, leaves Carlisle Citadel, its only halt, in June 1957 on its way south for its first run. It did the journey in 4 hours and 49 minutes.

From green fields to the largest marshalling yard in Europe. This was the start of work to the north of the city, levelling the site in 1959 for the Kingmoor marshalling yard. It never reached its full operating potential and parts of the site have since been re-developed by other businesses.

Progress at the Kingmoor marshalling yard in 1961.

The old Kingmoor yard pictured in 1959, showing the signal box and main lines passing through.

Enginemen at Carlisle Canal shed 1962 showing a coal hopper in the background.

Work starts to lift the rail lines at Kingmoor sheds after it was closed for steam in 1969.

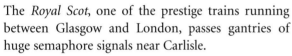

The *Royal Scot*, one of the prestige trains running between Glasgow and London, passes gantries of huge semaphore signals near Carlisle.

A new service seen passing through Carlisle Citadel station in 1967 saw British Rail carrying cars on waggons as the drivers travelled in carriages. The service ran between London and Scotland.

Photographed in 1966, this was the level crossing on Dalston Road with its signal box on the left. Always prominent in the city is Dixon's Chimney.

The rail line across the Dalston Road level crossing continued to Denton Holme, crossing the main road there until the bridge was taken down in the 1970s.

Looking towards the city, Wigton Road dipped down under this rail bridge which took the line from Canal Yard until it was demolished.

Pictured at the southern end of Carlisle Citadel station in 1966 is stationmaster Jimmy Leslie, the city's last stationmaster. The position was later superseded by that of area manager.

Lifting rail lines from the main Carlisle-Glasgow bridge over the River Eden near the Sheepmount to replace the steel girders with concrete beams in 1965.

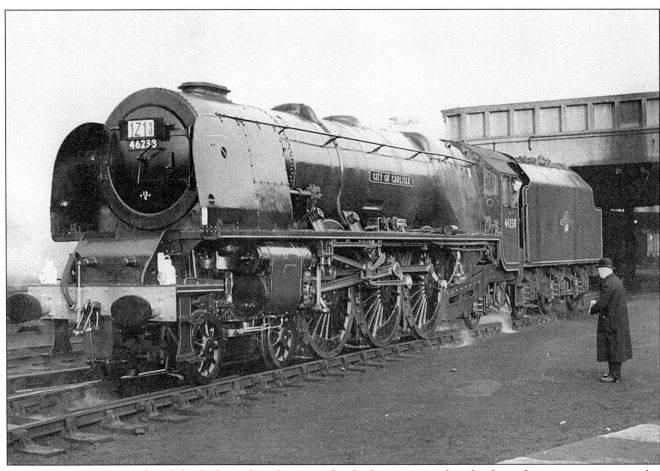

The Duchess class *City of Carlisle* which was based at Upperby shed was scrapped as the days of steam came to an end.

The city crest on the new *City of Carlisle* locomotive is unveiled by the Mayor of Carlisle Colin Paisley in 1995, accompanied by Denise Brown, business manager London Scotland InterCity West Coast.

Sir Nigel Gresley, an A4 class steam engine that has been renovated privately to run as a steam special, pictured in Carlisle station alongside a service Diesel in the 1970s.

In 1969, the first three Carlisle guards were trained as conductor guards, moving along the main line trains to check tickets as well as their normal duties. From left to right are James Brerton and Eric Fletcher (travelling ticket inspectors), Bill Atkinson (chief travelling ticket inspector in charge of the course), James Graham, Alexander Johnstone and James Turner.

The result of electrification to the railways, which was under way in 1972, is seen in this later picture near Carlisle station.

1995 brought the end of an era to the railways as British Rail handed over its lines to Railtrack under the first stage of rail privatisation. It was marked by a special steam run over the Settle to Carlisle line. The train is pictured in Carlisle with some of the crew.

Lord Inglewood (centre), MEP for Cumbria and North Lancashire, presents a certificate to Carlisle Citadel station manager Mike Kilgour to mark the station being judged second best in the country in 1994 from a total of 2,500 British Rail stations.

Engine driver and Mayor of Carlisle John Metcalfe (left) seen with the Dean of Carlisle, the Very Revd Henry Stapleton, and Tom Johnston, chairman of the 150 anniversary celebrations of Carlisle Citadel Station, at the unveiling of an artwork commemoration display following a special service in Carlisle Cathedral.

CHAPTER FIVE
On the Roads

The latter half of the century brought many changes to traffic and roads in Carlisle. One-way systems were introduced with the start of inner and outer ring roads. The M6 motorway bypassed the city in 1970 making one of the largest reductions through the city in traffic travelling between England and Scotland with a new bridge across the River Eden.

Early part of the century, a horse and cart makes its way leisurely towards Rickergate from Scotch Street.

A Carrs of Carlisle van delivers in the city during the first half of the century.

PC Edwin Mason is pictured on point duty at the junction of English Street and Devonshire Street in February 1941. It appeared in both the national and local press because it was the first time that the, then, only set of traffic lights in the city were switched off for two hours daily as an economy measure during wartime. It was snowing at the time and very cold on the feet so a kipper box top obtained from the nearby MacFisheries was used to stand on.

The island near the Old Town Hall which was used as a main picking-up point by city buses until it changed to West Tower Street after pedestrianisation.

A United service bus on the English Street to Botcherby route joins the rest of the traffic in Bank Street in 1968. The separate cab can be seen for the driver, with fares taken on the move by a conductor or conductress.

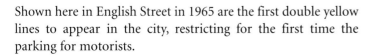

Shown here in English Street in 1965 are the first double yellow lines to appear in the city, restricting for the first time the parking for motorists.

The city's first traffic wardens take to the streets for the first time in 1967. From left to right are J.Bushby, A Robinson, E. W. Scaife, Janet Nugent, J. Kidd and D. Todhunter. Their initial brief was to advise road users on the rules with the aim of prevention rather than prosecution.

One of the busiest motor body repair workshops in the city during the 1960s was at James Bendall and Sons Ltd., London Road, where cars are pictured at various stages of repair.

Looking back towards Warwick Road, this was the Durranhill Bridge under construction in 1968. It crossed the Carlisle to Newcastle railway line at Botcherby and became part of Eastern Way, part of the outer ring road for the city which has never been completed.

Looking north from the Civic Centre in 1970, the construction of a new roundabout at Hardwicke Circus can be seen, and on the left the start of Castle Way which takes traffic behind the houses on Corporation Road, past Carlisle Castle and out to the west. This road was opened four years later.

Traffic from Scotch Street on the left and Lowther Street merges on to Eden Bridge at Hardwicke Circus in 1968.

Just near the route of the old Carlisle to Silloth railway line on Burgh Road, Ron Morton the car breakers is pictured in 1968.

Pictured with the Mini vans they used at the time on their patrols, the AA show off their new uniform introduced in 1969. The new dark-olive uniform on the right is shown off by patrolman Alan Wright as it is compared to the one it replaced, modelled by patrolman Michael Harrison.

Traffic in Botchergate in 1965 before the opening of the
Carlisle bypass.

Pictured just before it was demolished, this taxi rank in Court
Square at the railway station was used by official taxi drivers
as they waited for their fares.

One-way traffic is introduced to part of English Street, looking
towards Botchergate at the start of a new traffic management
scheme in 1968.

Looking north-east, progress can be seen on the M6 motorway bridge across the River Eden in 1969, part of the Carlisle bypass which was opened in December of the following year.

Tim Westoll (second left), chairman of Cumberland County Council, who officially opened the Carlisle bypass in 1970, is pictured with some of the project officials as crowds watch from the bridge at the Golden Fleece.

Mrs M. Paton and son Ross, aged three-and-a-half, watch the opening of the Carlisle bypass from the bridge above the motorway.

Pupils from St Gabriel's School, who had been doing a project on the new Carlisle bypass, watch the opening ceremony.

Now opened up as one of the city's main bus assembly points at the Market, West Tower Street, seen here in 1970, was once a narrow cobbled street with shops and houses. It is pictured looking from the bottom of Scotch Street towards Carlisle Castle.

West Tower Street in 1979, now one of the main areas for buses picking up and dropping off passengers in the city centre.

Carlisle city centre in 1976 during pedestrianisation around the Town Hall area.

Looking towards the city centre, this was the pedestrianisation of English Street in 1989.

CHAPTER SIX

The Best Days of Our Lives

In the latter part of the century, schools in Carlisle were improved with new buildings or extensions, comprehensive secondary education was introduced and the subjects offered really did make for the best days of our lives. From early school groups to unusual events, we can show only a small selection of activities involving pupils of all ages.

The first steel erection is in place early in the 1950s for the building of Carlisle Technical College in Victoria Place. Now offering a wider range of courses and facilities, it has since been renamed Carlisle College.

The Carlisle and County High School for Girls hockey team of 1943.

Pictured at the Robert Ferguson infant school Empire Day parade in 1938.

Walter Eite was headmaster at Robert Ferguson senior school for 31 years until his retirement in 1958, a few years after this photograph of him was taken. He celebrated his 100th birthday at his home in Dalston Road in 1992 when he was visited by a group of pupils from the primary school.

A class from Robert Ferguson School in 1940.

Pupils from Newtown School in 1955 with teacher Miss Bolton.

Grammar School pupils in their distinctive uniform who were prizewinners in the school year 1964-1965. The school later became Trinity with the introduction of comprehensive education.

Prizewinners from 1966 at the Carlisle and County High School for Girls. With comprehensive education it became St Aidan's.

In 1966 these were the pupils from the combined Creighton Margaret Sewell school who won prizes for their efforts during the year.

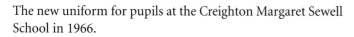
Prizewinners from St Gabriel's School pictured in 1966.

The new uniform for pupils at the Creighton Margaret Sewell School in 1966.

Ready for a new start, pupils at St Patrick's School, which was in Spring Gardens Lane on the site of Georgian Way, pack up items from their domestic science room as the school closed for good.

St Patrick's School was on the move in 1968 from Spring Gardens Lane to the new Newman School in Victoria Place, making way for the construction of the new Georgian Way. Newman School took pupils from both St Patrick's and St Gabriel's which was also closing.

Outside the headmaster's office at Harraby Secondary School where a noticeboard in the reception area reminds of the official opening on Thursday, 25 October, 1956. It is now the North Cumbria Technology College.

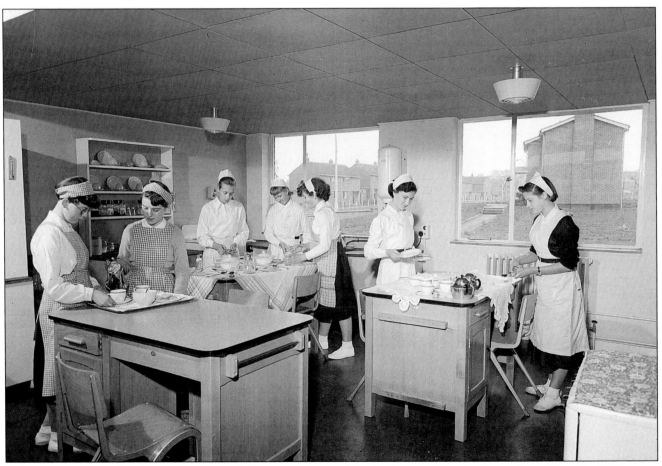

A domestic science class in progress, one of the subjects catered for in the new Harraby Secondary School in 1956.

Music is a popular school subject and here in the Market Hall, young musicians and the choir rehearse for the annual non-competitive festival in 1974.

In 1974 St Aidan's School set up their own television production using cameras formerly used by Border Television. It was used by pupils to make their own programmes.

After Carlisle started with its professional Rugby League team the game was introduced into primary schools where it was played by girls and boys. Pictured here are Rebecca Hudson and James Rooke from Kingmoor Junior School and the rest of the squad pictured in 1992.

Pupils from Inglewood Junior School celebrate winning the English Schools six-a-side soccer final which was played at Wembley football stadium prior to the televised England v Italy schoolboy international in 1992. Back row, left to right are Paul Reid, Terry Brown, Ryan Tulip and Ben Blair. In front are Jonathan Ashurst (left) and Brett Swift.

Newlaithes Junior School headmaster Howard Todd and staff join the winning British schools gymnastic team in 1994 on their return to the city with their trophies.

Belle Vue junior school won the city primary schools chess tournament in 1995. From left to right are Gary Ruddick, Mehdi Yazdi, Chris Blackburn and Angus Mitchell, all aged 11.

When Stanwix School held a pets' assembly, Katy Maiden, aged 11, took along her hamster. The assembly was held to promote animal welfare and the care of pets.

Just happy to be at school, Rebecca Smith, a pupil from Caldew Lea School, shows what the National Smile Week is all about.

Eden School headmaster Robert Gardner presents trophies to the winners of the last Eden Key race before the school was closed in 1993. The winners were Andrew Connor and Amanda Metcalf. The race became an annual event to commemorate the time during the last century when the school was the home of banker George Head, who forgot the key to open the bank and a messenger ran back to the house to get the key so that the bank could open on time.

CHAPTER SEVEN

This Sporting Life

Carlisle United have always been the main spectator attraction in the city but they have had their ups and downs from the burning down of their grandstand in 1953, promotion from the Third to the First Division, two Cup appearances at Wembley and in 1999 a fight to the finish to survive with a place in the Football League.

The Carlisle United AFC team of 1908-09.

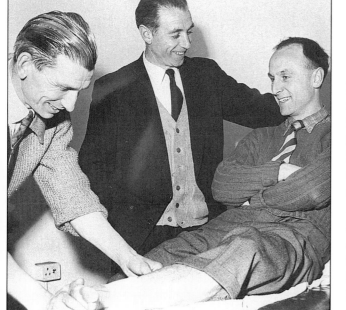

Ivor Broadis (right), one of Carlisle United's first international players, had two spells with the club, the first in 1946 when at 23 years of age he was appointed player-manager, the youngest manager in Britain. After moving to Sunderland in 1949 and then to several other top-class clubs, he re-joined Carlisle in 1955 for four years before moving to Queen of the South and then retirement in 1961. During the 1950s he was capped 14 times for England and played in the 1954 World Cup in Switzerland. At his peak he was recognised as one of the best inside-forwards in post-war football. He is pictured here during his second spell at Brunton Park with long-serving trainer Dick Young (left) and England team-mate Stan Matthews who was visiting the club.

There was a big shock for Carlisle United early in the morning of 11 March 1953 when two policemen noticed flames in Carlisle United's wooden grandstand. Even though re-inforcements were called for by the fire service, using a radio car for the first time, there was little left by daylight as the team started to arrive for training. The £6,000 grandstand had to be re-built.

Players could hardly believe what they saw as they arrived to search among the ruins of the grandstand in 1953, finding only a few shirts that had survived the flames.

Carlisle United's team of 1952-53, at the time of the grandstand fire, showing some stalwarts who played for the club for many seasons. Back row, left to right: McIntosh, Scott, MacLaren, Kinloch, Waters, Stokoe. Front row: Hogan, Alan Ashman (who returned later as manager), Whitehouse, Jackson and Drury.

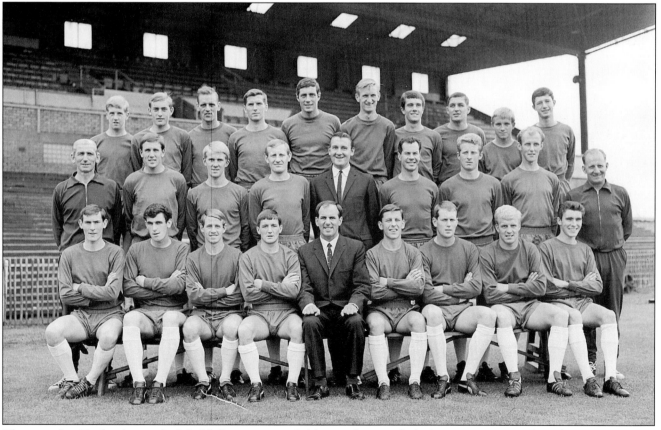

The year that England won the World Cup, 1966, and this was the squad playing at Brunton Park under manager Alan Ashman (centre front).

David Dent was club secretary for many years until March 1978 when he took up a similar appointment with Coventry before moving to the Football League.

In May 1974, Carlisle United celebrated their promotion into Division One of the Football League at a party given in Cumbrian Newspapers office, Carlisle, when everyone gathered to wait for the score of the final deciding game, Carlisle United having already played all their fixtures.

1974 and Carlisle are in the First Division, with teams like Manchester City, pictured here in September, visiting Brunton Park where Joe Laidlaw is seen challenging the 'keeper.

On 18 May 1992 Michael Knighton gave his first Press conference and took control of Carlisle United.

On a Sunday afternoon in May 1997, the Carlisle United team toured the city in an open-topped bus to a civic reception at the Civic Centre, seen in the background. They had beaten Colchester at Wembley in the Final of the Auto Windscreen Cup.

The crowd waiting outside the Civic Centre for the 1997 Carlisle United team to arrive.

The official opening of the International Bowling Tournament which was held in the city on 9 July 1919. The welcome was given by Bertram Carr (third right) who was the Mayor.

Liptons provision store in English Street had its own football team, pictured here in 1930.

The Carlisle City team of 1989, one of the teams playing in one of the many amateur soccer leagues in the city.

The Grammar School was a rugby union playing school and this is the team from 1943-44.

Carlisle Racecourse in 1966 during demolition of one of the country's first Tote buildings and the construction of a new enclosure. In the background is the main grandstand.

Gordon Richards (right), was one of the country's leading horse trainers, with many of his horses running at Carlisle. In 1984 however, racing enthusiasts flocked to Greystoke where he had his stables, to welcome National winner *Hallo Dandy*.

Wendy Burrell, pictured at the city's James Street baths, as it was announced that she had been chosen to represent Great Britain in the Olympic games to be held in Mexico in 1968.

Wendy Burrell, a 16-year-old pupil at the Carlisle and County High School for Girls, leaves her parents at Carlisle railway station on her way to the 1968 Olympic games in Mexico. She was coached by her father Jack each morning before school and every evening in the build up to the games where she represented Great Britain in the Ladies 100 metres backstroke. She was second in her heat and went on to the final where she finished fifth, the first European, in a time of 2m 32.3s.

The start of the Brampton to Carlisle road race in 1966 before the competitors reached the nine mile road section.

A photograph from May 1971 showing some of the lady competitors representing the Border Harriers at the Sheepmount, Carlisle.

In 1971, Ian Johnstone, aged 15, won the Collin VC Shield for the second year in succession during an athletics meeting at Gillford Park. The shield, which is for the local winner of a 100-metre handicap race, is awarded in memory of Lieut. J. Collin VC of Carlisle who was in the King's Own Royal Lancaster Regiment and killed in 1918.

Carlisle soccer referee Colin Seel, who moved from the sport locally to be a Football League referee for several years, pictured here in 1975.

A Border City Wheelers group from 1977 showing riders of all ages.

Carlisle cricket club team of 1979 playing in the North Lancashire League, pictured at Edenside. Back row, left to right: Robert Kilgour, Bimal Potel, Andy Forsythe, Jim Little, Kevin Reynolds and Dennis Murray. Front row: David Marshall, Willie Walker, David Musgrove, Mike Battersby (captain) and Albert Clapperton.

For over 30 years Tom Harrington has been one of the leading Cumberland and Westmorland wrestlers, holding world championships at many weights and picking up a lot of silverware from his sport.

Steve Brierley was a local player with Border Raiders, the Carlisle rugby league team which started off in the city in the mid-1980s before merging with Barrow in 1997.

Carlisle professional boxer Charles Shepherd brought top class boxing to the city in 1999 for the first time in many years, during two fights in which he first fought for the Super Featherweight Commonwealth Championship which he later succesfully defended.

Carlisle United needed to win the last game of the season against Plymouth at Brunton Park on Saturday, 8 May 1999 to stay in the Football League and in the dying seconds of the game even goalkeeper Jimmy Glass, who was on loan from Swindon, was in the Plymouth penalty area for a corner. It was his final shot, seen here, that gave United the goal they needed to survive relegation.

CHAPTER EIGHT

The Entertainers

In the late 1950s and 1960s, Carlisle had its share of top British and American singers live on stage, mostly at the Lonsdale ABC Cinema which was enthusiastically managed by Norman Scott-Buccleugh. At this time the new clubs in the city were also starting to bring in artistes with household names, but their demise and the closing of the ABC cinemas around the country left the city with few top shows until the gap was filled by the Sands Leisure Centre which continues to bring in top live shows.

The Carrs Works brass band of 1912.

The Revellers Concert party, pictured here in the 1930s, was based at Holy Trinity Church with help from John Sullivan who used to produce the Scouts' Gang Shows in the city.

Connected with amateur music in the city for most of his life, Frank Logan is pictured on the right of this group The Carlyle Four, photographed in 1932.

The Carlisle City Silver Band with some of their awards won in 1954.

The King of Skiffle, Lonnie Donegan, and Norman Scott-Buccleugh pictured at the Lonsdale ABC in 1957. The show ran from Monday to Saturday with 12 performances.

Singer Ruby Murray autographs records at E. T. Roberts music shop during her week-long stay in the city where she was performing at the Lonsdale ABC in 1956.

Dame Thora Hird (left), Vernon Gray and Janette Scott pictured in Carlisle during 1956 to tie in with the premiere of the film *Now and Forever*. The film was screened at the Lonsdale ABC.

Max Bygraves and ventriloquist Dennis Spice who were at the Lonsdale ABC for one week in 1957 with a near capacity audience for each show.

Scottish singer Kenneth McKellar signs autographs for fans Greta Graham (left) and Sheila Richardson in June 1960 at the Lonsdale ABC.

Cliff Richard (second left) and Lonsdale ABC manager Norman Scott-Buccleugh (third left) with other artistes at a performance in 1960.

Anthony Newley and Anne Aubrey made a personal appearance on the Lonsdale ABC stage in 1960 to promote their latest film *Let's Get Married* and are seen with the manager Norman Scott-Buccleugh on their arrival, when they were presented with a bouquet and a button hole.

The Lonsdale ABC cinema had a theatre organ in front of the stage and pictured here in 1968 Gordon Lamb gives a recital to other members of the organ club.

Mick Jagger of The Rolling Stones who topped the bill at the Lonsdale ABC cinema in 1964.

Local singer and Frankie Vaughan impersonator Rodney Warr is pictured at the One-O-One Club with Ann Shelton who was on a visit to the city.

Comedian Ken Dodd gave a performance in the Market Hall in 1970 and gets down among his audience.

Freddie Starr (third left) was at the Talk of the Border in Botchergate in 1970 where he is pictured with some of the clubbers.

Mick Potts (centre) with the Gateway Jazz Band pictured before one of their sessions in 1970.

Yheudi Menuhin, one of the world's most celebrated violinists, played at concerts in the city, and in 1971 changed his bow for a badminton racquet to play a little sport before his main performance. He died in 1999 in Berlin.

Dance and ballet were taught in the city by Florence Wilkinson, seen in the centre of this group taken in 1972.

Celia Baxter with some of her first ballet pupils in the city in 1972. She was a former dancer with the Sadler's Wells Opera Ballet and the London Festival Ballet.

Pupils from the Rita, Terry and Joy School of Dancing seen at a medal presentation in 1990.

Pat Allen pictured in 1976 with props for one of her shows. The Pat Allen School of Dancing has had dance classes in the Carlisle area for the best part of half a century, giving numerous performances for the public.

Carlisle-born opera singer Ida Maria Turri is seen on stage with the Royal Liverpool Philharmonic Orchestra in 1992 at an open air concert held at Carlisle Castle as a tribute to the 900th anniversary of the castle. The concert, which had an audience of almost 5,000, was the the city's biggest ever classical concert.

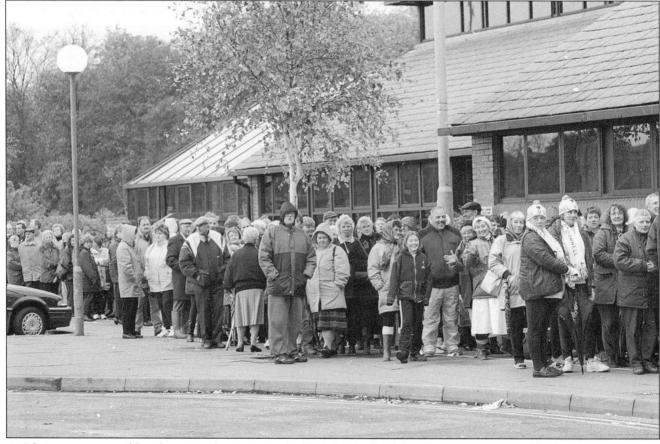

A ticket queue on a cold and wet October morning in 1993 for the Daniel O'Donnell concert at The Sands.

Pictured at the Market Cross in the city centre are pop group 911, whose music has reached the national charts including a number one. Lead singer is Carlisle's Lee Brennan (right) seen with the other two members of the group Jimmy Constable (left) and Simon 'Spike' Dawbarn.

Daniel O'Donnell on stage at The Sands in 1997, one of the regular performers there, always attracting a huge demand for tickets.

Robbie Williams on stage at The Sands in 1998, a former member of Take That and now a successful star in his own right.

CHAPTER NINE

It's All Happening

Parades and processions are all part of a city scene, sometimes sad, but mostly full of noise and happiness. From small gatherings in the outlying districts to the huge crowds of the revived Great Fairs, they have all had a part to play in the history of Carlisle and its people.

Making time for a photograph at Peace Day celebrations in 1919, held by St John the Baptist Church, Upperby.

The Earl of Lonsdale, the Lord Lieutenant of Cumberland, opens the 1928 Carlisle Historical Pageant in Bitts Park.

A large group of performers in Bitts Park during the Historical Pageant held in 1951.

The St James' Church anniversary parade in Denton Holme in the late 1950s.

At the Courts on 8 February 1952, the High Sheriff of Cumberland, Col. Tim Fetherstonhaugh, proclaims the accession of Queen Elizabeth II.

The late Sir John Burgess (second left), who became chairman of Cumbrian Newspapers Limited, seen with other officials viewing a model of the walled city of Carlisle at the opening of the Cumberland Newspapers historical exhibition in 1958. The model is now in Carlisle Castle.

Carlisle police constable George Russell was shot and killed while chasing a man after a housebreaking incident 1965, leading to one of the largest funerals seen in the city. A service was held in Carlisle Cathedral where the cortège arrived after passing 400 policemen and policewomen lining the route in Castle Street. The photograph shows the hearse following a lone piper in the Cathedral grounds.

As a tribute to George Russell, a stone carving of his head was placed among the gargoyles outside the Cathedral. The former Dean, the Very Rev. Lionel du Toit, and former Chief Constable of Carlisle, Frank Williamson, are seen at the ceremony.

A Civic procession at the cenotaph in Rickerby Park after the Remembrance Day wreath laying of 1966, showing the Mayor of Carlisle Gerry Coogan.

The dedication of a new war memorial in the Greenmarket took place in 1990, an event attended by the Duke of Gloucester.

A wooden cross is carried at the head of a Procession of Witness, marching to a united service in Carlisle Cathedral at Easter in 1969.

Everyone likes to follow a parade and these youngsters are no exception as they march with the Boys Brigade along Stanhope Road towards Dalston Road in 1969.

The Boys Brigade on Church parade in Regent Street, Currock in 1970.

Before the Cumberland Show, one of the city's largest annual events, moved to Rickerby Park in recent years, it was held in Bitts Park where this aerial photograph taken in the 1960s shows it in full swing spread out below the Castle walls in the top right.

The Mayor of Carlisle, Mr N. T. O'Reilly, is led from St Cuthbert's Church to the nearby Tithe Barn for its official opening in 1971 after extensive renovations.

Each year the Scouts held a St George's Day parade and service in the city. Here the parade and inspection in 1972 is at Carlisle Castle.

Cardinal Heenan arrives at the station to lead a procession to the Market Hall and the Civic Centre during a visit to the city in 1974.

In 1966, before the revival of the Carlisle Great Fair, only a gardener and a bus driver witness the Proclamation by the Town Clerk Bill Hirst.

In 1975 when a full programme of Great Fair events was re-introduced for the first time, there was a large crowd to watch the Proclamation and later visit the street market.

The finale of the 1975 Great Fair week was a parade of floats when so many spectators crowded into the city centre that it was difficult to pick out the parade. It is seen here in English Street.

In the 1970s Carlisle colleges held a Rag Week each year. These students dressed for the occasion are pictured at the Town Hall in 1976.

Queen Elizabeth II celebrated her Silver Jubilee in 1977 and street parties were held all over the city with over one hundred road closures. This group in Trafalgar Street are photographed below bunting strung between the houses.

A scene from Bonnie Prince Charlie, re-enacted at the 1977 Historical Pageant at Carlisle Castle as part of the city's celebrations for the silver jubilee of Queen Elizabeth II.

Melvyn Bragg, broadcaster and writer, marches from the University of Northumberland's Carlisle campus in Paternoster Row to the Cathedral to receive an honorary doctorate in civil law in 1994.

CHAPTER TEN

People at Play

Upperby Park, seen in this evening photograph, more commonly known by locals as Hammond's Pond, has for more than half a century provided a leisure area for city people and even some from further afield. Boating, a play area for children, caged animals, birds and a café could all be found there as well as gardens and a path round the pond for those who were just looking for a quiet place to walk. In 1999 the water was drained to carry out work which will improve the quality of the water, and at the same time the rest of the park is being improved, all due to a lottery grant.

This line-up of skaters in Upperby Park attracts a few glances from the men as they steady themselves for a photograph in late 1920s.

A day out in Bitts Park during Race Week, 1942.

Jennifer Sherdley (née Driffield) on the left with a friend at the suspension bridge in Rickerby Park in 1953, a background that looks remarkably the same today with the smaller bridge across the River Petteril.

Keeping cool in the River Petteril on a hot day in 1966.

Fun in the water at Upperby Park.

The arch of a railway bridge across the River Eden near Etterby frames these young fishermen and the former Carlisle Power Station at Willow Holme.

Gone fishing… three young children fishing reflect in the waters of the River Petteril.

Party time for the North Cumbria Association of Playgroups at Upperby Park in 1970.

A sunny day at Upperby Park as children enjoy the boat.

Music lovers relax in Bitts Park during 1977 at a pop festival.

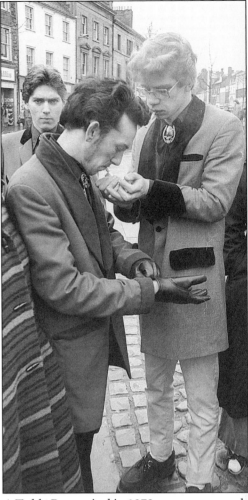

A Teddy Boy revival in 1978 as a group march from Victoria Viaduct to the Market Square to mark the 19th anniversary of the death of rock 'n roll singer Buddy Holly.

A permanent rail line at Upperby Park attracts enthusiasts, many of whom have built their own model steam engines, to give rides to children.

The start of the fun run section of the Cumbrian Run sets off from Crosby-on-Eden in 1990. The finish was in Carlisle where large crowds would turn out to greet the runners from this and the more serious competitors on the half marathon.

Competitors in the main section of the 1990 Cumbrian Run seen on the outskirts of Brampton just after the start, with almost 13 miles to go.

A new play area on the Raffles estate is opened in 1990 by the Mayor of Carlisle, Cliff Hayhoe, as he joins some of the football enthusiasts in the arena.

Rafting through Rickerby Park on the River Eden in a race from the suspension Bridge to Eden Bridges in 1994.

Anna-Leigh Taggart went along to the Morton Community Centre Teddy Bear's picnic in 1998 and had her face painted at the same time.

CHAPTER ELEVEN

Drinking in the Atmosphere

An early photograph of the Lorne Arms Inn, Shaddongate, before it was taken over in 1916.

At the beginning of the century drunkenness in Carlisle was so rife that the Home Office liquor control board set up the Carlisle and District State Management Scheme to reduce the amount of alcohol consumption.

In the early days of World War One workers in the Gretna munitions factory were being paid high wages and could find nothing more to do than come down to Carlisle to spend their time drinking in the 125 licensed premises. This added to the already serious problem and all the public houses were taken over in 1916 with managers put in charge under strict instructions on the amount of alcohol that could be sold to each customer.

The Scheme had its own works department based in Rome Street and carried out improvements to many of the buildings and interior decor. After some local protests, the 'experimental' Scheme, including the brewery, was wound up in 1971 and sold back to private enterprise.

The Light Horseman Inn at the turn of the century when there were 13 public houses in the short length of Rickergate.

The Farmers Arms Inn in St Cuthbert's Lane before the takeover.

In the Caldewgate brewery in 1966, showing one of the large copper vats.

The hop drying room.

Filling wooden barrels with beer.

Lorries photographed at the brewery in 1966 when the fleet covered 223,000 miles each year delivering to the pubs in Carlisle and district.

The start of local deliveries of beer in bulk started in 1967, shown here at the Malt Shovel in Rickergate.

Head Brewer Bill Monk with Alice Bacon, government minister responsible for the Scheme, at the time of her visit to the brewery in 1966.

Bill Monk, who came to the brewery in 1950, later becoming Head Brewer.

Norman Adams who came as general manager of the scheme in 1960.

John Marker, the last general manager of the Carlisle and District State Management Scheme.

The late Robert (Bonzo) Burns, manager of The Cumberland Wrestlers in Currock Street, was one of the go-ahead managers in the 1970s and 1980s who entered teams from his pub in all sorts of sports leagues and competitions amassing quite a collection of trophies.

The Cumberland Wrestlers football team of 1969, who played in one of the sports leagues organised by State pubs.

Darts, one of the pub games popular in the days of the Scheme. In the 1960s there were a thousand players taking part in the SMS darts league.

The Cumberland Wrestlers sign in Currock Street.

The unusual sign outside the Arroyo Arms at Harraby showing a solder drummer boy.

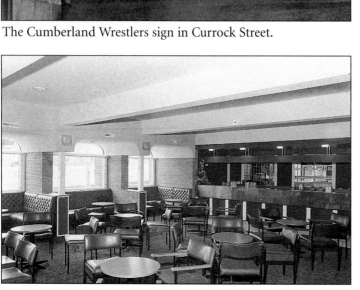

Inside the Border Reiver, Belle Vue South, after the opening in 1971, the last new pub by the State Management Scheme.

CHAPTER TWELVE
Leading Lights

Everyone looks forward to seeing a big event and there is nothing to beat a royal visit. Many of the royal visitors have been to the city more than once in the last 40 years, as have past and present Prime Ministers. Other international and national personalities have passed through the city from time to time, often unseen by the general public.

A royal reception in Rickergate in the 1920s for the Princess Royal.

A group photograph at St Aidan's Church in 1935 to mark the the Silver Jubilee of George V. All the youngsters received a commemorative mug.

Evelyn Wannop was the Stanwix School Coronation May Queen in 1937, the year of the Coronation of King George V1.

Celebrating the Coronation of King George VI in Ennerdale Avenue, Botcherby, in 1937.

The Mayor of Carlisle George Routledge walks with Princess Margaret in the Greenmarket in 1953 when the city was decorated for the Coronation of her sister as Queen Elizabeth II.

In July of 1958 Queen Elizabeth and the Duke of Edinburgh were due to visit the city for the octo-centenary celebrations, but the Queen was ill and the Duke came on his own, promising a future visit by the Queen. He is seen here in Castle Street with the Mayor Irving Burrow after a visit to Bitts Park where he was welcomed by huge crowds. On the right behind the Duke is the Lord Lieutenant of Cumberland, Sir Robert Chance.

As promised Queen Elizabeth and the Duke of Edinburgh did return to the city in October of the same year, and once again they are seen being escorted by the Mayor Irving Burrow, also near Castle Street.

Princess Anne visited the city in 1972 and is seen at the Cumberland Infirmary. Her visit also included the official opening of the new Cumberland Newspapers offices in Dalston Road.

The Queen walks to the west door of Carlisle Cathedral with the Dean of Carlisle, the Very Reverend John Churchill, to distribute the Maundy Money, a ceremony that takes place at a different Cathedral each year.

The Queen is seen in Carlisle during 1978 with the Mayor of Carlisle Jim Long and the Lord Lieutenant of Cumbria, J. C. Wade. She was here to hand out Maundy Money in Carlisle Cathedral.

Princess Diana came to the city to visit the headquarters of the British Deaf Association in 1983 and did her popular walkabout where she met some of the large crowds who had turned out to see her and give her flowers.

Again among the people on her second visit to Carlisle, this time Diana was with Prince Charles, the Prince of Wales, in 1986.

Prince Charles, seen in The Lanes shopping centre.

In 1993 the Duchess of Kent opened the new Eden Valley Hospice in Blackwell Road and is seen being shown around by the first matron Margaret Dunn.

Prince Edward arrives at Carlisle Airport in 1996 on his way to present prizes at the Duke of Edinburgh Awards Survival competition which was held at Greystoke Castle.

Sophie Rhys-Jones pictured in the background at Carlisle airport in 1996 during an official visit to the county by Prince Edward. The couple were married in June 1999.

Princess Alexandra inspects men of the King's Own Royal Border Regiment at Carlisle Castle where she presented Bosnia medals.

Politician Herbert Morrison photographed in Carlisle where he was the main speaker at this meeting in 1952.

Labour party leader and former Prime Minister Harold Wilson on his way into a meeting in Carlisle College, Victoria Place, in 1975.

Conservative party leader Margaret Thatcher speaks to some of the crowd outside the Civic Centre during a visit to the city in 1976. She later visited the city again as Prime Minister.

Prime Minister John Major speaking from the steps of his electioneering bus in the centre of Carlisle in April 1997.

A very brief visitor to the city in the early 1960s was former American President Dwight D. Eisenhower photographed in Carlisle railway station as the north-bound express stopped for just a few minutes.

In the 1960s French film star Brigitte Bardot arrived at the Crown and Mitre Hotel late in the evening for an overnight stay on her way to Scotland, but was displeased that the Press had gathered and soon left to continue her journey.

Bill Roach, who plays Ken Barlow in the television soap *Coronation Street*, is pictured in Carlisle in 1965 when he performed the official opening of a shop in the city. During the first British Soap Awards which were televised in May 1999, he was the recipient of a special achievement award for being the longest-running soap star, having been in *Coronation Street* since the first episode in 1960. The presentation was made to him by Cumbrian broadcaster and novelist Melvyn Bragg.

Disc jockey, TV personality, wrestler and marathon runner, Jimmy Savile passes some slower walkers in Botchergate on his John O'Groats to Lands End charity walk in 1971.

Having been chosen as Miss World in 1974, Helen Morgan's first engagement was to a toy fair in the Carlisle Market Hall. She arrived in the city on top of the world as she posed for photographers outside the Citadel station.

By evening time in the Crest Hotel, Helen was in a more thoughtful mood and resigned before disappearing from the media for several days. It was eventually revealed that being an unmarried mother and also a connection with a divorce case was the reason for the decision.

CHAPTER THIRTEEN

Military Links

Carlisle Castle ensured Carlisle's early military links, with a later army presence at Hadrian's Camp and Durranhill. During World War Two there were several airfields in the area including one at Kingstown which is now an industrial estate, and until the end of the 1950s a Naval base at Anthorn. There was also a Royal Air Force Maintenance Unit (14 MU) on the northern outskirts of the city which closed in 1996. Carlisle Airport, formerly Crosby, survives as a commercial airport run by the City Council.

Sitting on the front left of this group from 1914 is Harry Zeller, a member of the Cumberland Artillery, just before their involvement in World War One.

Edward Wheatley Pigg, who was secretary and later managing director of Teasdales in Westmorland Street where this photograph was taken, is the driver in this World War One photograph. He used to meet wounded soldiers at the Citadel station with this ambulance team and take them to hospital.

Munition workers photographed between 1914 and 1918 at the Drill Hall in Strand Road.

Members of the Cumberland County Council ARP photographed at Scotby during World War Two.

Jos Graham (second right, back row) was a driver instructor on Bren Gun carriers in 1940 and is seen here with one of the classes in Mary Street, Carlisle, where three of the tracked vehicles were kept in an otherwise empty car showroom.

National Service Group No. 54.13 at Carlisle Castle in July 1954 at the start of their two years National Service.

Field Marshall the Viscount Montgomery of Alamein stands in the back of his army car as he drives along English Street towards the Town Hall to be made an Honorary Freeman of Carlisle in 1947.

Seen in 1959 at Carlisle Castle are the Colours of the 3rd (Militia) Battalion and the 4th Battalion The Border Regiment just before they were laid up at a ceremony in Carlisle Cathedral.

Sir Fergus Graham, Lord Lieutenant of Cumberland, inspects soldiers at the Castle at the final parade of guns of 851 (Westmorland and Cumberland Yeomanry) Field Battery RA (TA) who ended a 100-year association with the city due to re-organisation of the Territorial Army.

The meeting place for personnel from all the services, the NAAFI in Rickergate, is pictured in 1966, just before demolition after the opening of the Civic Centre which is seen in the background.

The wartime airport at Kingstown which is now a trading estate.

The Army Apprentices College was set up at Hadrian's Camp where in the 1960s many young soldiers were introduced to army life and trade training before moving to various regiments. Here a group pass out in 1962.

In 1969 a thousand people in the Market Hall saw Group Captain E. G. F. Hill receive the Freedom of the City on behalf of RAF 14 MU, from the Mayor of Carlisle Mr J. J. Bell. It was the Golden Jubilee year of the unit in Carlisle, the event ending with a march past and salute by the Queen's Colour Squadron at the Civic Centre. RAF 14 MU closed in 1996.

The Colours of the 4th Battalion The Border Regiment (TA) are laid up at a parade on the Castle square in 1974 ending the final chapter in the history of The Border Regiment.

An informal photograph at the Castle in 1978 of RAF personnel and the Green Goddess fire engine 'Miss Piggy'. The military fire engines were in use during a firemen's strike for more pay.

One of the Green Goddess fire engines brought out of storage and into service during the strike.

Old comrades march past the new cenotaph in the centre of Carlisle during the 1993 Remembrance Day service.

The French drums captured at the battle of Arroyo dos Molinos in 1811 pictured at the farewell parade and beating of the retreat at Carlisle Castle in 1994 for the King's Own Royal Border Regiment band, which was disbanded in August of that year.

A general scene at RAF 14 MU in 1996 at the official closing down ceremony of the unit.

CHAPTER FOURTEEN
At Your Service

From an early police motorcycle escort to the latest technology in answering emergency ambulance calls, this chapter shows how we rely on public services every day of our lives.

Police motorcycle escorts pictured at the Cathedral in the 1950s. On the left is Joe Richardson on a Royal Enfield, with Dick Cowen on his Norton.

Police on parade at Carlisle Castle 1962 for their annual inspection.

Armed police appeared in the city several times in the 1990s, and are seen here in 1993 at the Crown Court in Warwick Road.

City fire-fighters demonstrate an early fire pump in front of one of the current fire engines in 1976.

A city fire engine leaves the Warwick Street fire station in 1966.

A city fire engine from 1970.

One of the most spectacular fires in the city was during 1972 when Penguin's factory in Denton Holme required the evacuation of people from surrounding houses. A fire-fighter is seen here high above the flames at the height of the blaze.

The Penguin factory on fire above the adjacent houses.

Smoke billows from a different part of the Penguin factory.

Residents start to move their belongings out of their houses as the factory fire rages.

Scott's Leather works are seen engulfed in flames in Rome Street, dangerously close to the Carlisle gas works in 1973.

A series of fires in disused property in Botchergate in 1997-98 resulted in the road being closed or restricted to traffic as fire-fighters dealt with fires or had property made safe. This photograph was taken in 1998 at the Portland Centre fire.

Pictured at Willow Holme alongside the River Eden is Carlisle Power station which supplied electricity until the end of the 1970s.

The gas works in Rome Street, photographed from one of the storage cylinders in 1969. Production of gas was stopped two years later when it was eventually piped from the North Sea.

The ambulance section of the Civil Defence demonstrate mouth to mouth resuscitation at an open day held in 1966.

In 1968 the two main parties on Carlisle City Council (Labour and Conservative) made an agreement with a mayoral 'Magna Carta' which decided on a system of selecting mayors of the city. The manuscript was held by Eddie Scambler, municipal correspondent of *The Cumberland News* and lasted for some time, stipulating that the majority group should have two successive mayors to the minority group's one. From left to right in the Civic Centre with a backdrop of photographs of a hundred past mayors are Hugh Little, Cyril North, Eddie Scambler, David Hamilton and J. F. Wood.

A photograph during the early part of the century of the judge's car waiting for him at the east door of the Cathedral.

A rare photograph in a courtroom, the last sitting at Carlisle Assizes in 1972 where the court had been held since 1811.

Viscount Whitelaw (fourth left), former MP for Penrith and the Border, opens Carlisle's new £9.5 million Crown Court complex in Warwick Road in 1992.

The guests in the main courtroom at the official opening of the new Crown Court complex.

The modern control room in Carlisle for the Ambulance Service pictured in 1997.

CHAPTER FIFTEEN
Weather Watch

The earthquake of 1979 was the biggest surprise of nature that could ever have hit Carlisle, but the shock waves in the early hours of Boxing Day, although felt all over the city, caused little damage. More frequently floods have submerged low-lying areas of the city, and Rickerby Park in flood is still an annual feature which follows heavy rainfall in the Eden valley.

A photograph from the early part of the century when Caldewgate suffered flooding which spread completely across the road.

There was an unusually heavy fall of snow in the city centre during 1946, shown in this photograph which features the Town Hall and the snow-covered Steel statue which has since been moved to the top of Bank Street.

A picturesque view of the centre of Carlisle in 1953 showing the island that used to divide English Street, with the old Town Hall on the right.

Upperby Park, or Hammond's Pond, photographed after a fall of snow has covered the ice in 1962.

It's just not cricket. Carlisle's cricket pitch at Edenside is covered with flood water in 1967.

Looking down Greystone Road at the junction of Bowman Street in 1968.

Vehicles move slowly into town along Warwick Road during the 1968 flooding.

Rain was so heavy in 1979 that stall holders in the Market needed to be mop up before customers could be attended to.

The earthquake that hit the Carlisle area on Boxing Day 1979 was centred about ten miles under Longtown and reached five on the Richter scale. Most damage to property was in the Warwick Road area of the city where firemen are seen on the roof of a house there. A chimney stack and roof are seen to be damaged.

Also in Warwick Road, David Klein is seen with masonry that has fallen from his house.

A boat is launched to carry out a sheep rescue on land between Warwick Road and the River Eden in Rickerby Park during the January floods of 1982.

The flooded road outside the old brewery on the road into Willow Holme in 1982.

Brunton Park, Carlisle United's football ground in Warwick Road, is covered in ice after flooding in January 1982.

One of the first places to flood in the city is Rickerby Park where the River Eden bursts its banks allowing the water to spread over a large area between Brampton Road and Warwick Road.

Early morning snow in 1997 caused huge traffic delays, this queue of vehicles seen in Newtown Road.

Relaxing in Bitts Park during a spell of sunshine in 1978.

The paddling pool in Bitts Park is always a favourite with the children when the sun comes out and they can splash about in the water.

CHAPTER SIXTEEN

Telling Your Story

Since the 1960s, newspapers have been joined by local television and radio to inform and entertain the people of Carlisle. New technology has brought colour to both newspapers and television while radio is able to give regular news bulletins to listeners.

English Street in 1953 showing the *Cumberland News* office.

Well-known faces around the city in the 1950s, this group of Carlisle journalists were photographed at an NUJ dinner in 1956.

A line of linotype operators in the English Street *Cumberland News* office in 1966, with Alan Byers on the nearest machine.

Pages being made up when *The Cumberland News* was produced at English Street, prior to the move to Dalston Road when a change from hot metal to web offset printing was made.

Princess Anne leaves the new Cumbrian Newspapers headquarters in 1972 after she had officially opened the new building. Behind her is the late Sir John Burgess, who was chairman of the company.

The Cumberland Newspapers editorial department in Carlisle soon after the move to the new headquarters in Dalston Road in 1971.

There were soon computer screens on every desk as *The Cumberland News* continued with its lead in the use of technology. This shows the reporters section of the editorial department.

Looking at the new Comet Press which she officially opened on 5 November 1998 is Lady Burgess accompanied by her son Robin, CN Group's Chief Executive. The Comet press in the new press hall brought the latest in printing technology to the company and increased the quality and amount of colour that could be used.

Workers from the *Carlisle Journal* return to West Walls in Carlisle in 1967 to find the inside of the building totally destroyed following an overnight fire. The weekly newspaper continued to publish until 1969.

Before the opening of Border Television in 1961 the 1,000 foot high aerial was erected at Brocklebank above Caldbeck. The photograph shows the base and the start of the metal construction work.

Guests pictured at the official opening of the Border Television studios at Durranhill in 1961 just before the first live transmission.

Mary Marquis, one of the first announcers on Border Television.

Derek Batey is known nationally for his programme *Mr and Mrs* but in 1965 he also presented a series of programmes to find Miss ITV. He is seen here with the contestants for one of the weekly heats.

The Cartner twins from Carlisle returned to the city after working and training at the BBC to join Border Television, Alan (right) working as an announcer and Bill as a studio cameraman. They are seen in the studio in 1977.

A photograph of the new transmitter which was brought in to use by Radio Carlisle (now Radio Cumbria) in 1975.

Hospital Radio presenters photographed in 1979, broadcasting to patients in Carlisle hospitals.

CFM Radio in Carlisle celebrates its first birthday with John Myers (centre) who launched the station, Darrell Thomas the general manager (left) and Paul Evans who was one of the presenters.

CHAPTER SEVENTEEN
Wonderful People

Here we meet just a few of the Carlisle people who have had stories to share in the last half century.

This photograph which was taken in 1896 is typical of many family groups taken around that time. The eldest couple is William and Catherine Moffat (née Hills) who are seen with members of their family at 53 Ashley Street. The Hills family, in the early 1800s, had a shoemaking business in Castle Street and were freemen of the City of Carlisle.

One of Carlisle's famous characters was Jimmy Dyer, a violin player who is featured by a bronze statue in The Lanes shopping centre. He was also a great walker and this small snapshot is understood to have been taken of him by John Jardin on the outskirts of Carlisle.

The baby in this photograph is Patricia Paterson, who was the last to be christened in St Mary's Church near Carlisle Cathedral on 31 July 1938. The church was demolished in 1953. Now Mrs Kelton, she was born in Bird-in-Hand Lane in Castle Street where Rufus House now stands.

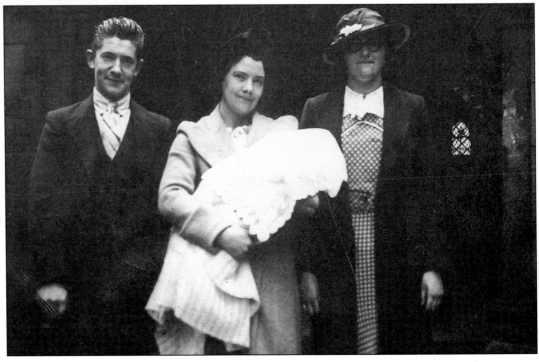

St Mary's Church near the Cathedral which was demolished in 1953, having not been used for some time.

Well-known in the city for his driving school, Reg Brown is seen with one of his first cars, a Ford 8, in the 1950s. He later ran a fleet of cars and instructors as the number of car owners grew.

Carlisle has had three sets of triplets during the last half century who have made occasional appearances in our newspaper on special occasions in their lives. The first of these are the Wroe triplets, June, Christine and Rita, who celebrated their 50th birthday in 1996 but are seen here in their first school uniform.

The Westmorland triplets Carol, Gill and Joanne, two years old in 1970.

Ruth, Anne and Christine, the Holmes triplets, pictured in 1981 at their first birthday.

Pictured at the corner of Bank Street and Lowther Street in July 1956 is Billy Dixon, whose shout of 'Not Many Left' still brings a smile to the faces of passers-by. Once a farmworker who was hired at the annual Town Hall hirings, he has become a personality in town, having been Town Crier at the revived Great Fairs, but always a newspaper seller for *The Cumberland News*.

Miss J. C. Carter was the matron at the City Maternity Hospital in Fusehill Street for many years, a well known face for many Carlisle mothers. She retired in 1972.

Pictured her in 1950, Dr F. W. Wadeley was organist and choirmaster at Carlisle Cathedral for many years, being made a Freeman of the city in 1966 just before his retirement.

Knife sharpening in close up…

This knife sharpener was often to be seen around town with his pedal operated circular sharpening stone. He is pictured in English Street in 1964.

Joe Brisco had a horse sanctuary at Blackwell for many years and in the 1960s turned much of his effort into giving a good home to pit ponies who were being turned out of the pits at that time.

Well-known personality, jazz man and owner of Todd's Mill which included Dixon's Chimney, Mick Potts (left) is seen at the top of the chimney with *Cumberland News* photographer Jim Turner in 1970 when steeplejacks were working on it to reduce the height to 290 feet.

Chris Bonington (left), one of the country's leading climbers and conquerer of Everest, stands on top of Dixon's Chimney in 1998 with *Cumberland News* photographer Phil Rigby to publicise the paper's Heartbeat Appeal to raise £100,000. The 290-foot high chimney was being fitted with steel bands to strengthen it and had a ladder running up the full height.

Carlisle-born writer and national newspaper columnist Hunter Davies pictured in the centre of Carlisle in 1974 on one of his returns to the city to autograph his latest book.

Margaret Forster, author wife of Hunter Davies, pictured in Carlisle in 1996 at Carrs Biscuit Works (now McVities), the subject of one of her books about Carlisle life.

Pictured in 1968 with his fox mascot, George Baxter, or Twinkletoes, appeared at all the Carlisle United matches at Brunton Park and many away games too.

Not a local-born player, but certainly adopted by Carlisle United football supporters is Peter Beardsley, who is seen at Brunton Park in August 1979 just before playing his first game there. He went on to play for various Premiership clubs and England.

CHAPTER EIGHTEEN
Into the 21st Century

Into the Millennium, a look at building developments and lifestyle that will take Carlisle into the year 2000.

The new Cumberland Infirmary building, still under construction in 1999.

Pictured from the roof of the Civic Centre in 1999, work on the new Debenham's site can be seen, making an extension to The Lanes shopping centre which can be seen in the background. The new road which replaces East Tower Street can be seen in the forground.

Work in progress during 1999 inside the new style Covered Market which will include a first floor shop.

After the fires of 1998, part of Botchergate has now been demolished, with plans for re-development that would complement other work already started. This view is the site of the former Simmons furniture shop and Odeon Cinema (formerly The Botchergate and Gaumont) pictured from Portland Place.

One of the new developments in Botchergate's former Co-op building is the Woodrow Wilson, a modern pub and restaurant bringing the first revitalisation to the area.

David King, pictured at a meeting held in the Sands Centre to discuss the Carlisle Millennium project which was to consist of glass structures in Castle Street, part of the cost paid for by the National Lottery Millennium Fund, the rest by the council. Mr King has been able to show a lot of opposition to the plan with the result that it is now under review by the new Conservative-led council, although work is now, in 1999, well under way.

Following local elections in May 1999, the Conservatives became the majority party on the city council for the first time in 20 years. New council leader Mike Mitchelson is seen on the site of the Millennium Pyramid at Tullie House in Castle Street.

Mobile telephones continue to get more popular in 1999, with new shops opening up all the time. Here are Beth Davies (left) and Lucy Bowes with the latest models.

Digital equipment is, in 1999, being used extensively as technology progresses quickly. At Border Television, Broadcasting Minister Janet Anderson is seen with managing director Paul Corley as she commissions the new digital control room.

The Internet is increasingly being used for business and pleasure by people of all ages, and this is seen particularly in schools all around our area where pupils like Anna Hamilton (left) and Marissa Birnie make use of the new service.

Just as it was at the beginning of this century, Carlisle's most visible landmark, Dixon's Chimney, will see us into the Millennium. Now strengthened with steel bands it is in good order to stand for many years to come. This photograph is from Kendal Street.